# The Eagles Should Have Been Far-Seeing

# The Eagles Should Have Been Far-Seeing

A Journey to Forgiveness by

Virginia Towne

© 2025 Virginia Towne. All rights reserved.
This material may not be reproduced in any form, published,
reprinted, recorded, performed, broadcast,
rewritten or redistributed without
the explicit permission of Virginia Towne.
All such actions are strictly prohibited by law.

Cover design by Shay Culligan
Cover image by Wesley Towne
Author photo by Virginia Towne

ISBN: 978-1-63980-767-3

Kelsay Books
502 South 1040 East, A-119
American Fork, Utah 84003
Kelsaybooks.com

*This chapbook is dedicated to my mother. Thank you for loving me so fervently, despite and beyond the horror of your childhood. I am sorry I could not save you, and I hope you have finally found true peace.*

# Contents

| | |
|---|---|
| Suicide Note | 11 |
| Stardust Core | 13 |
| Family Tree | 15 |
| Bright Things Yet | 18 |
| The House | 20 |
| Ghosts | 22 |
| Postpartum Depression Elegy | 23 |
| Moments Like Glass | 25 |
| Hang the Moon | 27 |
| I Handle My Children | 29 |
| Blue Lake | 31 |
| Where the Tall Pines Are | 33 |
| Ceremonial | 35 |
| Lakota Oyate | 38 |
| To Give Up | 40 |
| Honor | 42 |
| I Love You Again and Again and Again | 43 |
| Speaking Truth to Power | 45 |
| Rivers of the Heart | 47 |
| Old Wooden Swing Set | 48 |

# Suicide Note

"The eagles should have been far-seeing,"
Was the last apocalyptic note she scrawled
In her broken and trembling hand,

Words that I tried so hard to understand.

What eagles?
What sight could they have beheld
That might have brought back to her
A reasoned light to illustrate
Something other than her tortured mind
Worn fragile and thin by monsters
Who starved, and beat, and raped,
A child?

Or would these brave and noble birds
Have donned armor in her defense,
Flocking in hordes to peck out the eyes
Of those so vile that they would welcome,
Just to destroy,
The spirit of a foster child?

Or did these eagles nest inside her womb,
As like a sweet salvation,
My spirit bloomed
For them to lift on soaring, golden wings
And place gently in her arms,
A child more precious than the moon
And all its diamond light,
Since in my tiny form she found the strength
To chase away the memories,
To hold back a schizophrenic night?

So, it was these birds who were short of sight,
Who gave a gift and flew away.

Abandoned in her time of need,
Her mind crumbling from the weight
Of something from which she was never, truly free,
Little by little, she disappeared.

And though we tried so hard to save her,
No one was strong enough:

Not even me.

# Stardust Core

Though she once,
At the moment of her birth,
Shone with immeasurable light,
Unadulterated, unremitting, unashamed,
Breaking the barriers of time and space,
Wide-eyed emerging into that very first day,
Unwrapping the shadowed arms of the other side,

Though she proclaimed
*I am here!*
Like the brightest star,
Speaking with her spirit alone

Having not yet lost
The language of God,

Though she was at that moment
Lifted into her place,
Embraced by vast, light-laden arcs
Cast just right,
A speck of hope within the wide
Galaxy of life,

Though she emerged bright
And sure;

She fell.

She plunged through a darkness that stole it all,
Light years of cold,
Voices that battered the
Stardust core
Of her soul,

Until one day,
At the edge of some endless abyss,
She turned and tried to find her own star
Amongst the farthest
Reaches of the night sky,
Eyes seeking in the black,
And at last perceived the faintest glow,
A tiny spark from so many, many years ago,
A remnant of a little girl she once knew.

Alas, the pain was just too far
And the cruel wind slapped at her reaching arms
And so she just stepped back and let herself fall

Away,

Away from the light,

Away from it all.

# Family Tree

The vague shadow of an ancient oak pulsing
Like an image through static,
Through drifting fog
So thick that only the wind
Can lift it and let slip
The outlines of
Where I began.

My ancestry is incompletely buried.
The sharp rocks of drunken nights
Slice upon the roots
Disfiguring, pummeling, smashing,
Rendering mute
The stories their craggy hollows could tell,
Dissolving in that same fear
My grandmother must have known so well.

I don't know how to find her,
To reconstruct a broken form
From all of these pieces,
These fallen leaves that
Drift like secrets,
Like the ones my mother
Whispered to me in the dark
When I was nine and old enough
To hold them, to hold her,
When she fell apart.

Because they took them, you know.
My mother, her sisters, her brothers,
The county clipping the roots like
Plucking flowers,
Like it was nothing at all to scatter
Children in the wind,
Like fallen leaves upon the shallows
Of some lonely pond,
Like broken branches
Overpowered by a system that
Only wanted them
Gone.

It wasn't just the wind that raped the tree,
But a system that decided
Whose voice to wipe away and
What to keep.

My ancestry is incompletely buried.
Sometimes, I'm sure I can hear her sobbing,
A broken, fragile song, emerging from the earth
Just where the roots, interlocking, stop
The dirt from completely blocking
The story of a battered woman
Buried for too long.

The vague shadow of an ancient oak pulsing
Like an image through static
Through drifting fog
So thick that only the wind
Can lift it and let slip
The outlines of
Where I began.

What if I run my hands along the bark,
The broken pieces, the empty spaces,
Where her voice might be?

Grandma, speak to me.

# Bright Things Yet

Yes, it is true.
Sometimes, I am eight.

I stand by the mantelpiece and watch the clock tick upon the wall.
Each second seems excruciatingly extended.
Is there really a purpose to these
Endless days that stretch into years,
That stretch into meaninglessness?
She rests in bed again.
Depression shifts itself into the corners of her room and her smile
Does not reach her eyes.

Mom is very tired.

My father gently guides me from the room,
But she draws me back to say
"You know I'll love you,
Even when I'm gone."

I run outside and throw a vibrant red ball into the sky,
As if to stubbornly defy her

Hopelessness.

I so want her to see that there are bright things yet.

I dig them from the ground with my hands
And find them in the remote groves of pines
That stand in harsh wilds
Outside the boundary lines of
The sadness drawn across her eyes.

As a young child,
I wanted to shatter that sadness with light;

Yet, now it is I who
Has to fight the darkness in my veins,
Using all of my strength to push it away
From my children,

So they do not have to do the same.

# The House

The house that I grew up in is a faded red
Because the bricks have basked in the
Tortuous sun of
My memory
For too long.

The house that I grew up in is a pile of sand
Because they knocked it down
After my father died,
Like the flesh
That falls away
From cancer.

The house that I grew up in is two places, really:

A favorite dog,
A small fence
That holds my swing set and a flower garden
And I am five and shouting
Look how fast I run, mommy.

And I am twirling and twirling and the garden and the grass and all
The faces whiz by like a film reel on fast forward
And when it stops only

Four cold walls.
Painted white and waiting
For me to run my hand along them and walk into
The blue-toned master bedroom,
With the old oak mirror
That reflects only
Empty space.

These faded hues of memory,
These hollow chambers,
Sit upon my chest like
A house made of brick and sand.

# Ghosts

I cannot ever truly love but
Fail. I call out now to silent graves.
Prayers cut rivers down my face and
I ask them to rise, rise, rise,
Spread fragile wings and fly!
Lift, like vibrant monarchs against the sky!

But the stars are a deaf glory
Across a moonless night
That cannot speak,
And these tears they only fall,
Dropping heavy and useless to the floor.

I am bleeding from the very tributaries of my soul,

Cry these words out into the stillness of the room,

And I thought you might hear.

I hold your picture to the beating of my heart,
But there is only silence
And the endless, imperceptible wall.

You are just too far, too far, too far.

I am an utter failure;
Calling out to ghosts who were
Never there at all.

# Postpartum Depression Elegy

Afterbirth; the tangled sinews of blood beating through
Hollowed veins
That once pulsed with more volume than the mother river
Before the killing flood.
Because the Yellow River broke
In a raucous torrent of salt and sediment
Meant to nourish life
I should have known!

Afterbirth; the extracted remnants of my own creative process
That once sculpted with more artistry than a tsunami
Off the Indonesian coast
The face of life.
Or death.

But my baby lived!
Like the glorious beauty of the Gold Macaw
Opening its gilded feathers over a Brazilian canopy,
Like the gentle song of the Meadowlark
Through the first buds of spring,
Like the sweet breath of the wide-eyed fawn
Under her mother's breast,
Our love lived so entirely.

Before the felling of the wood.
Before the bitter dust that
Suffocates the memory of a lush beginning.

After birth; the second coming.
Yeats speaks it perfectly because
The beast comes lumbering.
His breath a stinking, choking, crying, rank
Evaporation filled with
Emptiness.
His warped claws digging, pawing, slicing
Mutilating that pulsing cord that
Tied our hearts together.
A destruction like no other.
A massacre.
A natural disaster.

After birth; the echoes of what should have been.
Like the falling tune of bright and feathered birds
Perched in the carcass of some wood,
Singing a death song
For all that used to be. For all I used to be.

After birth; something that emerges,
Like the she-wolf ducking furtively between the
Burning scrub
And out onto the fertile plains she runs!
Then turns, beckoning:

Come here you hellish Sphinx
And bring your desert birds!

I am a Phoenix rising,
Pulsing, beating, shaking,
Like the glorious afterbirth that drums the song of those that fought
And won.

# Moments Like Glass

As I get older, there are some things that are
So precious
I can barely contain them in my soul.

Moments, encased in glass as thin as fly paper.
A single harsh movement, or a careless thought,
Can shatter these.

Like when you touch the toe of your boot
To the delicate crystals of ice
Spread out across the sparkling grass
In the midst of a mild November frost.

How quickly they dissolve!

How quickly they leave you reaching for a memory;
A pattern you can never reconstruct,
Like building enchanted forests out of dust.

Mostly, these forests are of love.
My children's laughter in the morning,
Their footsteps beating like
Tiny hearts against the floor.

My son, growing strong, yet still reaching with toddler arms,
"Mommy, up," and at bedtime,
Little voices calling, "Mommy, love you more."

Moments, encased in glass as thin as fly paper.

I am afraid to touch them in my mind.
I am afraid of the needle of time
That will shatter these,
Melt these,
Dissolve these into memories
So precious that I will try with all my strength to conjure them
Back to life,
But as I get older,
I recognize their flight.

# Hang the Moon

I have tried my best for you, my babies.

I even bought the moon
And nails and screws.
I found the rusted hammer in the shed
And tapped and tapped the crescent edging
Until it halfway stuck.
You sat by me
And stared with wide expectant smiles
As I tried to hang the moon

And yet, your eyes they told me
That the cold, dull metal was not
Quite right
And your excitement faded.
"It does not shine
Like the one outside, mom!"
I know it does not shine
Like the one you wanted to
Find in your spacesuit made of
Hefty bags and a salad bowl hat.
That one would have superseded all
Of your expectations.
That one would have matched the vibrance of your dreams
But I could not replicate it.

And sometimes the moon falls down
And twangs against the floor
And now, we don't live with Daddy
Anymore,
And the little world you knew as home
Was flung as far away
As the moon.
And I try
I really try
To explain why it had to be so.

But sometimes,
I sit on the edge of this worn-out bed,
A crooked crescent
Dangling cheaply above my head;
A counterfeit,
It mocks me,
"You tried,
You tried,
But you know they are not satisfied
By what you have to give:

An insufficient replica of the perfect
Mother's love."

# I Handle My Children

I handle my children as if they might disappear.

Sometimes when I am holding them,
My face pressed to their hair,
My hands around their little fists
Like so many eagles
Cloak their nests
In feathered wings,

I feel their edges start to blur
As if pulled by a strong hand
Through a silver curtain.

"You can't have them!"
I yell at the space above their heads.
"They're mine!"

And yet I feel the weight of being gifted
So many treasures that
I don't deserve,
That I try to earn.

I handle my children as if someone might come back for them.
Speaking to me sternly, they will explain
"These are too precious, too rare,
For you."
But I would not let them go.

I would come for them.
Charging like a lioness
I. Would. Come. For. Them.
Through every burning flame
And every mangled wreck
And sterile hospital bed,
I. Would. Come. For. Them.

Dragging both legs
And seeping blood
And holding the heart
Inside my chest
With my own two hands
I. Would. Come. For. Them.

I would die for them.

I handle my children as if they might disappear.
Clutching their tiny bodies and all their edges,
Holding them in, keeping them whole.

# Blue Lake

By the shores of an alpine lake
Newly thawed
Sun bright and full of an early summer's
Hopefulness,
I watch the goslings waddle
To the lapping edge of the water.

Their mother eyes me, but
Notes that I am
Not a threat.

And I am not a threat.

I tell her softly that she should pass
And I will not throw rocks
Or chase her off
Like so many do
As if we have some greater claim to this
Blue lake
And the evergreen forests
That surround it
Than all of the wild things that quietly adjust their days,
Trace a slightly wider arc,
Around the cacophonous noise we make,

Before slipping quickly up, up and away
Into the thickness of a wilderness
Rife with ponderosa pines
And a crisp silence
Broken only by the wind

And the bird songs
That are the first to speak
Of the winter's end.

And I prefer to listen
And look often
To the farthest contours of the foothills against the sky,
Borne away from even my own voice that
Seems to demean the purity of things
Free and wild.

And time,
A gentle drifting
Like a body on the surface of the lake
Drawn out to the center when
The tide is just right
Pulls me away from these cities we make
Inside our minds
To justify the way we think our lives
Mean more than hers;

Just a mother leading her young ones to take a drink,

And I will never stop her;

*The spirit of honest things.*

No, I hand her my heart to take to the center of this
Blue lake
And let it sink like a rock to the dark,
Cool depths where it belongs,

From whence it came.

# Where the Tall Pines Are

Up in the hills where the tall pines are
Just along the rippling creek
Where the cut banks rise high
In rough granite faces and the eagles glide,

There is something I have forgotten and
Left far behind in the remote corners of childhood,

Something just beyond where the water
Carves into the rock,
Within the beating heart of the mountains,
And above,

Inside the infinite, blinding sky.

I remember breathing in the taste of wonder in the clean, alpine air,

Watching my father cast his line,

His tall figure at ease with the gurgling flow of the mountain
 stream, and I,
Blending into the forest winds,

Leaving an imprint of myself in case I should return again.

Today, she stood with me along the edges of the turbulent waters
 that polish the bottom rocks.

Her five-year-old fingers held mine.

She pulled me along the banks, laughing.

Did you see it?

Just for a moment,
In my eyes:

A child in an unnamed, unbroken place,
Watching the dipping of her father's line

Into the waters of a moment
Forever suspended between the mountains of time.

# Ceremonial

There is such thing as a healing round.

I won't explain in detail as
A person does not speak of
Sacred things,
As if to assign form to what is
Better left
Shifting through the wind,
Like the breath of God.

Better left to those whose
Ancestors passed down the songs
That shall not be sung in winter.

But I will speak of the
Splitting of my skin
At a feather's edge
Bone whistle call,
Walls dissolved
And all the grief came pouring out.

Bent over, arms clutched across my chest,
Sobbing now,
Tears wet the earth.

I finally allow in
The presence of my mother's death

And a broader mourning
That I cannot define.

There is such thing as a healing round.

I am walking now
Footsteps quiet on the cathedral floor,
Faces in stained glass
Watching from lofty spires of marble
And slick, gray stone.

Do their eyes follow my small, hesitant form?

I do not frequent churches and prefer to come alone

To enter a silence
In which all of the suffering
That this world
Has ever borne
Hangs heavy
Suspended in the resonance of
Great, imposing halls,
Vast oceans of sorrow, and here too,
Something that carries and lifts;

Perhaps, the love of God.

There is such thing as holy ground.

The water knows
Rushing between the rocks,
Between the wild, greening cliffs
Where gently a little Robin flits
And perches on the tangled brush
Beside the shore.

You belong here, she sings,
You belong
You belong.

# Lakota Oyate

Lakota Oyate, you raised me,
A rootless, tender-hearted girl,
Kicking up the dust on an
Empty reservation road.

Lost, but found
In your kindness.

Tiwahe, when I had none.

I filled my plate at your tables,
Wojapi and thickened breads,
The laughter of the wild-hearted children
Ringing through the stars like
The songs of rainbow-chested prairie birds.

Little ones, how you grasped my hands and
Claimed me.
How clearly I can hear them calling,
"Auntie, auntie, come play!"
And so, the people of Paha Sapa,
The rivers, and the plains,
I love you, thechihila,
Forever.

My little children will forever walk in kindness and humility
Because of the values you raised in them;
Because you drew them in
As if they were your own blood.

Because you sewed vibrant ribbons on their shirts
As if they belonged in their humanness,
In their innocence,
To your great nation.

Lakota Oyate, I can never repay you
For the way your heartbeat

Saved me, prayed for me.

Pilamaya Wopila,
Mitakuye Oyasin.

## To Give Up

The great arms of the cottonwoods release fragments of themselves
Across the evening sky,
As if the edges of clouds could
Lift from the flutter of leaves
And drift out and away,
As if giving up fragments of oneself
Is soft and easy,
Like the bend of the river
Around the greening banks
On a gentle summer day,

Like giving up is not brutal
Or bones cracked on the cold tile of the
Bathroom floor
When you can't even do this anymore
And there are tears laid around you like bright
Flowers of pain
Spilled and wilted and dried up again
And you curl into yourself
And simply wait for
The end.

There is a giving up in that roughness and there is a giving up in
The radiance of the sun
Emanating from the warm rocks
At the edge of the cliffs,
Lifted off the backs of the verdant hills,
And there is a giving up that is a gift
And not an acquiescence.

And thus it is,
Like the river's edge,
I give up this familiar space
To the flooding of the rains;

Take the banks of all I know
And allow their swift erosion
Down to the vulnerability
Of my soul.

I give up the strongholds
Of dread
And cast these crafted layers to the edges of the stars

And I won't give up the openness of my heart,

Or the way I can see so far
Across this wild, limitless wilderness
Of tangled greens and thick, rich
Muddied growth.

Just by the river,
Hope.

# Honor

*for my husband*

I speak with my own voice,
But at my shoulder,
An unconquerable army,
Quiet, ready.

And that army is his heart.

# I Love You Again and Again and Again

*for my husband*


I am safe here,

With your inked hands tracing up and down my spine
And my cheek tucked against your neck,
The fan above us undulating in dark space,
A whoosh, whoosh repeating
With each breath you take and

The music lightly plays and plays.

You tap the drumlines against my
Shoulder blades
And hum softly
With your face against my face

And I am safe.

And you tell me
"There are not enough words
To say how much I love you,"
And it is like my heart falls right
Through my skin
And I say I love you
Again and again and again.
I curl up and let you hold me like a precious gem.

It is only time that will betray,
And it only time that can wrench you away,
And even then,
I will fight each dying day,
And like your seeking hands along my spine
Under blankets streaked by a
Distant moonlight,
I will seek you across the river
To the other side
And hold your spirit
Safe in that forever night.

# Speaking Truth to Power

Gandhi's Satyagraha or
Foucault, speaking truth to power,
Articulate a certain bravery,
Like a fearless April flower.

She breaks through the cover
Of hardened snow that wants to hold
The northern plains in stasis,
Forever, never letting go;

Yet, how delicate her petals
Open to the radiance of the sun,
Shining with a valor that belies
The fragility of her stem.

Ah, but she is not afraid
Of breaking!

Her truth is like molten iron,
Solidifying in the blinding light
Of every new morning.

She wears her colors without shame,
Heralding the dream
Of summer,
Like a lonely soul that
Still clings tightly to the image of some wild lover
That she may never hold.

Sitting here in the grass beside her,
I want to thank her for being bold;

You see, I know,
A last, triumphant, colorless, cold
Will kill her;
Yet, even in brevity,
The rich vibrancy of her prophecy
Gives us all

Hope.

# Rivers of the Heart

Ah, this mountain river!

The fragile banks erode and
Crumble into sorrow,
But the sun glints off the surface still each morning
And there is solace in the shining.

Could that brightness really be mine,
After everything I should have done
That might have changed the arc of time,
Words I could have said
That would have left
Certain hearts alive?

I haven't fought all the right fights
And some beautiful things have died
Right here in my hands,

But I think there is a chance
That these waters still run true.

The mountains stand unmoved,
After all.

And the rivers of the heart rush and fall.
They rush and fall down the rocks and

They are still pure.

## Old Wooden Swing Set

Flying on an old wooden swing set
Green paint peeling off the sides
Sunlight descending through the spaces between the leaves
Thick on the branches of the old oaks
I never thought I would
Leave behind.

She's kicking high now
With spindly legs
And tipping her face upside down
Laughing like a child
Should
Laughing though life would
Place a sadness in the world
Little by little.

I walk through the edges of the garden in a different time
My voice is hers and mine.

I will always love you
Hopeful little thing
Trusting that these ropes will hold forever
Looking back at four walls that will never crumble
But they did
And they do
And you knew, you always knew.

And if you could only hold onto one solid thing
And if you could just be bright enough to save everyone,

And isn't that why you were always smiling?

Such a happy child.
Such a happy child.

And I want to tell you it is ok to stop smiling
And it is ok to let the swing fall down from the sky,
And it is ok that things die right there in the middle of the light
You try to bring.

I love you, anyway,
And I will swing beside you
And hold your hand and we can lay back our heads
And laugh and laugh and laugh
And maybe that will finally

Be enough

And I can forgive myself.

## About the Author

Virginia Towne lives in the beautiful Black Hills of South Dakota with her husband, Wesley, and their (almost) Brady Bunch of five children. She holds a BA in Anthropology from Cambridge University and an MA in English from Indiana University East. She is an English instructor for Oglala Lakota College, a small tribal college located on the Pine Ridge Indian Reservation. Virginia writes poetry predominantly as catharsis and as the exploration of both joyful and traumatic experiences through imagery and the music of language. Her greatest wish is that her poetry might make someone else feel not quite so alone. This is her first chapbook.

www.ingramcontent.com/pod-product-compliance
Lightning Source LLC
Chambersburg PA
CBHW070942160426

43193CB00011B/1784